ENGRAVINGS

Isaiah 49:16
"Behold I have engraved you on the palms of My hands..."

RUTH FIONA CHEAL

Ten|16
PRESS

www.ten16press.com - Waukesha, WI

For information, please contact:

Ten|16
PRESS

www.ten16press.com
Waukesha, WI

To The Engraver

Introduction to ENGRAVINGS,
a book of praise, prayer, pain, and promise

The Reader will notice the use of British English spelling throughout, and place names, flowers and countryside depicting southern England. The Author is English and retains a deep love for her native land although now living happily with her family in Wisconsin USA.

Most of these poems were written between 1995 and 2015 but they are deliberately not presented here in chronological order. They span times of great joy, peaceful contentment, depression, and deep sadness. The idea is to lead you through the emotions, onwards to the steadfast assurance of security and love in Jesus Christ - available to everyone. Each person experiences some losses and sorrows which colour life; it's up to us to choose the colour:

we have the choice to rejoice or we can refuse to choose

In spite of devastation and disaster Habakkuk chose to rejoice in the Lord. He took his eyes off his troubles, knowing he was powerless to control events, and instead he continued to look to God, who provides surefooted confidence through the bad times and the ability to see the colours of joy!

Truly Second Sight

If I had eyes but could not see or had no eyes at all
How could some friend describe for me the wonder of it all?
No help from camera or paint,
Colors blurry, lines too faint......
Words the only option left
To lift from feeling so bereft
So words! Ring true and do your best,
Sound out the spectrum east to west,
Create with vibrancy sublime
In every phrase and every line
The best that human praise can do
Giving credit where credit's due
To the One Who first spoke words
Spoke into being creative words
Giving us inner eyes, and choice
To see Him everywhere and hear His voice.

Pauline

Who upset you, who so horrid
As to make you seem insane?
Was there no one there to help you
Through unkindness, fear and pain?
Now you're marked a schizophrenic
Sad, unlovely, lonely soul.
I sat beside you, helped with washing,
Patient listening was the goal.
You blew raspberries, pulled rude faces,
Acting like a weird recluse,
Shouting, swearing, yelling, shaking
Giving views of past abuse.
I learned a lot from conversations
Yes, even from your silent rage
And your angry revelations
Were not easy to assuage.
You plus your voices have grown around
My heart in some strange way.
I shall miss you Pauline, Pauline
And hope your brother comes today.

Oh God My Children

Oh God my children......
thank you for shielding them as they have grown
continue to keep them in hands that You own
although they've been mine but only on loan.
You give hope from past hurts to new healing
gaps closing, rifts mending, revealing
fresh chances more layers ripe for peeling.
Tears for the blank years of fatherheart bled
tears for what *should* I feel now dad is dead?
Tears for 'I can manage alone' - with toss of the head.
Tears for soul searching solitude, aching emptily,
tears for 'Surely this isn't how it's meant to be?'
Tears for that ghastly phrase dysfunctional family,
Oh God Your love......
tentative tears for freedom and quiet rejoicings
still they flow, getting better, flushing toxins,
what might have been, what might yet be voicings.
Tears for fence-mending, gap-bridging warm smileys
wasted years craving hugs and trusted apologies
good tears for new love's committed promises,
tears of happiness, wonderment, new groom, new bride
tears for sea-changes, life-stages, heartbursting pride
tears Jesus for Your everlasting arms open wide.

Listening

Listen
to what the tears have to say
where do they spring from
why do they flow so freely
welling up from deep places of pain
from unwellness they surge

Listen
hear what the heart is crying
the soul also calls
what is there left to look at
peering through blanketing fogswirls
pressing heavily in

Listen
hear what the Lord is saying
His words never change
why do I doubt His meaning
thinking He's too busy elsewhere
adding guilt to distress

Listen
Oh God are You listening
can You hear me struggle and strive?
Break through the smothering fog
pull it from me so I no longer choke
let me bask again in Your sun

I AM listening!

Sluggishness

Went for
      a walk after rain
         grey sky rinsed pale
      came across
the horns of dilemma
   - a snail
         (they hide in the dry but love damp, wet or gale)
     his mate up ahead
       who with sad
          silent wail
    had passed from a crunch
 to a smear on the trail
(really don't know if 'twas the fe or the male)
 repulsive
for sure
     but that's to no avail
      we shudder
and squirm
 at this
    silvery
 tale.

His Promise

The afternoon walk that day was unhurried
Soft mud slipping, flinty chalk tripping
Anchored on tufts of wet grass in the track.
Dazzled by diamonds on blades at my feet
Matched by gem droplets on newly bare trees
Equalled by sun-glare on Newhaven sea.

Climbing the Downs always worthwhile effort
Every step improving the view as you turn
Enhanced by majestic cloudscapes above.
Clouds blown eastwards west and north to south
Shadows gracefully leapfrogging valleys
Up-swooping, darkening sheep on the hills.

That day those clouds rolled over Mount Harry
Heavy and grey, nearly black, full of rain
Low over Lewes, then, transformation......
Behind me the sun burst forth from the west
Turning clouds even blacker - perfect backdrop
For the rainbow, stunning, brilliantly jewelled!

First just a portion, foreshortened by cloud
Then sudden completion, perfection, and awe
Colours so luscious all else paled away.
Unbroken dome joining Neville to Caburn
Was suddenly mirrored - a second bow near,
Oh what a delight, and a double one too!

Dear Lord You made it just for me that day
(there was no one else around!) the Downs
Were mine - as is Your ancient promise, Lord. Thank You!
Jeremiah 10:12-13; Genesis 9:12-16

Helping Hands

Yes I lift my hands in praise to You
That's the least that I can do
When I think of what You did for me
Your hands pierced and bleeding on the Tree
O Lord please show me how I can
Use hands to help my fellow man
Small ways, insignificant may seem
But even there Your love is seen
Not for me large gestures grand
Unless by Your grace I understand
That any small thing I do or say
To help another along the way
Using my hands, or feet or voice
To encourage another to want to rejoice
If one more soul can enter Your glory
That's surely the point of this short story.

The Black Door

The black door;
partly opened partly closed
was it really black or
did her mind just paint it so?
Memories come flooding but
she keeps trying to forget.
Oh God please supply the courage
and a friend to hold her hand
so that door can be pushed open
and the hurts faced yet again, tho'
this time as an adult, facing pain
humiliation, childhood fear.
Wasn't going through it once, enough?
But no, it wasn't only once, it went
on for years and years - and no one knew
or seemed to care. No maternal interest
no paternal questionings - where have you been?
Left to her own devices she discovered
all his vices and what he liked to do to girls
behind that big black door.
Lord take her hand and push that door wide open.
Hold her while she looks with covered eyes.
Surveys the wreckage of her early years and
manages to breathe again and shed some tears.
Lord as the crying heals so the healing cries -
Cries out in anguish, how can I forgive?
Impossible, quite impossible without
your love oh God - so pour it down, wash
that black door and all it used to hide, so
it can now forever stand open, open wide.

On A Beach In Wales

Sun's low radiance warms my wind-whipped perch
a rest from lengthy walking.
Eyes up to distant downpour drenching working 'mills
(to some folk a necessity, to some a ruined view)
heaving white-capped seas reflect clouds' changing moods
from pewter grey through plum to deepest green and on to
storm-dark mauve a sudden backcloth for stunning 'bow of every hue
in perfect arc - ancient promise ever new - marvel briefly then it fades.
Drink in fresh vistas where land meets ocean, whose hand but God's
can hold those boundaries in place? Land as it stands and
tides in constant motion.
Eyes down, drawn to surfing spume disturbing smooth expanse
fresh washed clean of all but the Creator's touch.
Momentary gap in gathered cumulus above turns shimmering sand to blue until
local lords descend on red-legged busyness of aggressive argument - the fight
for gritty treat or morsel on the wing.
I too find treasures: a starfish - on a northern beach in Wales?!
Salted glassy fragments - slicing edges nicely nulled;
a cleft of pebbles held fast twixt rocky neighbours who perchance
claimed one to start but every ebb adds to it;
huge boulders with embedded past exposed, announcing their white fossil'd shells
were once indeed life-filled;
green slate protruding unobtrusively from 'weedy pools;
wet corrugated sand in rippling mode like roof of canine mouth;
horizontal trees in flat relief on wetter sand where mini deltas flow.
And so much more, more than words can show.

Similarities

Hard, cold & brittle, wet when dredged, clam'd tightly shut, and tough
but fragile, cutting, jagged-edged externally dull & rough.

Oyster or person - or is it both? interesting similarities -
unhappy person surely loath to see oyster as it's meant to be.

Humans & oysters both start small, soft & unprotected,
one should toughen & grow tall, one for a pearl's elected.

It's only when a grain of sand gets thru the shell's closed sides
that the oyster understands his hard work - or he dies.

Spit & polish he must make to coat that sandy grain
cover it so it will not irritate, again, again and again.

That iridescent coverup in layer on layer then forms
the pearly gem that man digs up soon female neck adorns.

Which proves appearance can deceive - if oyster's unattractive shell
hides beauty & in dark conceives a jewel whose worth man knows well.

Now when we meet a person who seems hard & cold, in pain,
perhaps without an interview we'll see her sandy grain,

and know that under brittle shell she's got intrusive hurt
maybe we could help her dwell on future pearls, not dirt.

When God grows oysters in their shells what lessons He'll unfurl -
deep within each human dwells the potential for a pearl!

Whether we can see it there matters not at all, God does,
we must believe, though life's unfair, He sees pearls in each of us.

If we let Him He will change our grainy imperfections
transforming them - how wond'rous strange, adding to His pearl collections!

The Nightmare

My son, my son...... the dream... I woke, but what a waking,
Nineteen years and more have passed
Since he emerged -
So pink and perfect, white crowned with peachfuzz
Deep blue solemnity in unblinking stare
As we introduced ourselves
The prolonged pain of his arrival then
Close parallels the pain of absence now, 4000 miles away
Though, just as then the cord was cut
Some self-sufficiency began
So again it had to be, to grow into a man.
No human legs are strong enough to straddle the Atlantic
Without much strain and aches and pain- the enormity gigantic
In my dream I bridged that gap and went in search of him,
Asked the uncles, aunts and friends
Family, college dean, employers, "Where is he?"
"Oh, not here, these past few months -
We thought he had moved on." "To **where??**"
I called and called and paced the streets
With heavy heart and growing dread......
Finally, in hovel indescribable
That whiteblond hair identified
The quiet, gruesome form, arm needle scarred
Outstretched from bone-thin ragged pile
Deep blue anguish in unblinking stare
And one last sigh, "Oh Mum, where were you?"
I woke as in my arms he died..... I woke, but what a waking

*Oh God please watch over my son, keep him close to You, let him be that
one sheep that You'd delay the other ninety nine for, while You go hunt for
him: treasure him Lord, and hold him in the palm of Your hand.*

Why Weepest Thou?

Again last night; I wept again
so much crying; impassioned rain
tears for past mistakes and pain

tears for repercussions of sadness
tears for you Lord, Your almightyness
and splendour, Your strong tenderness

and love. Tears too for my bitterness
the deep horrors and just plain unfairness
of life - inspite of which, Your steadfastness

tears for passing time and great changes
tears of anguish & remorse over bad choices
tears of rejoicing over hope and good choices

tears of wallowing in what-ifs and if-onlys
weeping for unknown what-might-have-beens
tears of praise for Your patience and rescues

mostly just the well-controlled sniffing
as a few drops round the eyes swimming
and hang from the nose between dabbings

but sometimes the pressure has built up
to such an extent that it erupts
causing hasty retreats which seem abrupt

it's physical pain as the heavings
and gut-wrenching sobs and the howlings
release those long suppressed feelings

noises heard from equator to arctic
enough tissues to fill a large basket
it is none-the-less very cathartic.

Concrete Blocks

Concrete blocks with rough-hewn edges
erect themselves between you and God
impenetrable, cold dark lonely.

Several times you heft hammer and
chisel, exhausting attempts
to create chinks of light,
frustrating.

Suddenly peering through
one small chink you see
that He too with chisel
is working His way
towards you!

Yes, He is still
there waiting
to help you
dismantle
the blocks
as soon
as you
will let
Him.

Prison

Walking past the prison wall
the inmates' voices can be heard.
Within the confines of the brick
the guilty, free to shout, play ball
but ever watched by guard and clock,
must, when hour's up, return to cell.
Stripe shirted men while out of doors
have opportunity to see
high on their wall, perched gingerly
a bird, who's plumage in the wind
is ruffled, balance kept by claws
securely clenched, head on one side.
But do they see? And if they do
they surely envy feathered friend
it's freedom to vacate the roost
and fly away, wheel, twist and bend
riding thermals above the Weald
along the river and Downland field......

For the convicted and condemned
there is no real freedom......

Unless they turn to Jesus Christ accepting His free gift of love
with forgiveness for mistakes and sins,
thus enabling the forgiven to become forgiving.
Then even though their bodies still must stay incarcerated,
their heavy hearts and darkened minds will see the Light, and with it find
their spirits free to soar above the wall in God's own freedom, best of all.

Cancer Cannot

She smiled when she saw the ad
From the Cancer Research Campaign
They too, celebrate year seven-five
May they go on a long, long time!
Tho' more tears flowed she smiled again, she won't give up while still alive!

Knowing she'd been given just two
Or three more weeks at best, to live
She decided then and there she'd
Make the most of each day granted
Do everything she could to give those around her and yes indeed...

Anyone who read her journals
Later when the final curtain
Draws, glimpses of her dying heart.
Battles of denial, anger
'Why me, God?' - thoughts uncertain, fear and anguish tearing her apart.

Friends prayed for healing, tried to cheer,
Doctors, nurses, did all they could,
Pills and injections when the pain
Pushed her beyond, quite past bearing.
It was then she knew that Jesus would be beside her, like sun through rain.

Cancer might destroy her body
But she knew without a doubting
It couldn't eat away her peace
Nor dim Christ's radiance in her;
In silent prayer - no breath for shouting, let others follow, finding release.

Masks

10 Leyton Square sounds rather smart
but it's not.
Independent now, "I do as I please,"
so she says.
Social Services call it after-placement care,
where's the care?
Two sad children -she's got the boyfriend in,
playing grownups.
She's quit her job, he's on the dole, they
seem fairly happy.
Got it sussed, they claim, no worries,
who needs a job!
Down to the 'center they sign on for work
then cry wolf
claim a crisis loan, get a new TV or phone.
What parental hearts are breaking or
have broken? These adult looking kids
or are they childlike adults, with their
sad pathetic masks firmly on, hiding
co-dependency and pain, bravely
camouflaging unshed tears.
What are they running from, or to?

Poor Jenni

Poor Jenni wrote from prison such a tale of sad defeat,
Her addiction to the filthy muck King Heroin hoped she couldn't beat.

There are prison bars of all kinds and gaolers keen to throw away the keys;
Cells of fear as well as concrete, steel bars of hatred no one sees.

If for you it's not King Heroin then perhaps Queen Pornography,
Or the chains around your heart are forged from bitterness maybe.

Whatever has you in its frenzied grip, be it booze or greed or lust or coke,
If the need for it is your daily bread, you know well addiction is no joke.

May I introduce you to another King? King Jesus is His name and in His hand
He holds the keys to unlock every cell, and longs for you to understand...

That He offers freedom and release! He can break all chains that bind you
Be they nicotine or food; His peace can still your cravings, His love is
Unconditional - **all you have to do is ask.**

Waiting

The waiting hall at any hospital
must feel the same, chairs line the
walls, old magazines abound
and green plants of some description
stand sentinel in dried out tubs,
surveying all and keeping watchful eye
upon the people: sad and mostly
frightened, some in pain and some confused,
all wishing they were somewhere else.

Each time the double doors swing open
unclenching airlock with a sucking sound,
blessed welcome cold comes surging in,
a brief refresher in that stuffy clime.
The admin staff are over stressed
though doing sterling work with medics
who must nobly smile for every patient.
If only, oh if only they could all be introduced
to the Great Physician personally!

The waiting game of life would then
no longer feel the same but reveal
deeper meaning to each accepting soul
whose confusion, fear and tensions could be released,
exchanged for comfort hope, assurance and real joy!

Memories

Those hands, now so thin and cold,
Lying unused, not useless......
Hold one and think -
Not so long ago those hands
Gripped trees for climbing
A pole for fishing,
Then, tentatively at first,
Reached out to touch a girl
Then surely caress a wife
And on to clasp an infant
With such love and pride.
A job of work for pay
Was done, as well as
Chores around the home,
Those hands were seldom still
Except in sleep.
Maybe raised in prayer and praise
Or maybe unaware of God.
But now, as if in death,
Those hands in lap lie resting,
Tissue paper skin, blue veined, shaky,
Boredom not age alone responsible.
Life just still flows but no one knows
Or seems to care when ebb will come.

Conversation

O God - forgiveness - what a word
it's quite impossible, how can I pray while full of hurt?
I can't, no good at all.
What is this thought that's crept right in…'don't believe I want to'…
there now, that's really honest, have I shocked even You?
May I still talk with You O Lord - well isn't that what praying is?
I do want conversation Lord so an answer would be nice…
it's two-way communication, please God do answer me.

What? Oooh that's hardly fair; but You are God and it's Your job…
all right, now I can see -yes, You have forgiven me
so who am I to shout and cry 'I can't forgive' - no, no.
No, not alone I can't, that's right, so now I'll ask for help -
Please will You help and hold my hand
and hold at bay my pain; no, better yet, please take away
the angry thoughts still rife, and in their place please
would You fill, yes fill me with Your love.

Leaving no place for hate to grow, then keep reminding me
that following Your footsteps means forgiving as You do.
What's that? Not just once You say but seventy time seven
and even more may need to be…
let me get through once first!
O God - forgiveness - what a word, did seem impossible
but now thanks to You not quite, not easy either but
possible at least; stay with me Lord, help me see it through.

Horizons

horizons
greeny blue
grey silvery hue
hazily
lazily
lifting the eye
from chocolate chalk
of downland ploughed
but April rain
is changing
greeny blue
with silvery hue
as germinating
seeds push through
turning chocolate chalk
to spring green grain
interspersed
with rape harsh yellow
and flax blue smoky mist
interchanged
as wind and cloud
chase dark to light
and back again
while over all
larks flute liquidly
the Creator smiles

Swimming at The Pells

Hurried humans do not frown,
watch my fluffballs golden-brown,
eleven ducklings - they're all mine
says mama, quacking them in line,
keep away from sluice gate drain,
it's full and gushing 'cos of rain
you my babies are mighty fine,
I'd hate to lose you any time,
little experts in the waters,
how I love my sons and daughters,
don't dart about, stay close to me,
there's a heron near that tree,
dog on the loose, boy with stick,
you must learn and do be quick,
your papa's gone, now comes that swan,
hurry, up into the lawn,
gather round and do not worry,
better to be safe than sorry,
danger's over for a while,
go back and swim, make people smile!

First Year in College

When busy in Bible School oh my dear friends
It's obvious and now I do see,
Though it may be hard going from start to end,
It's the right place for us to be!

No baths till seven, no lights after eleven -
Just how many rules can we bend?
Cleaning dishes and loos - a far cry from heaven
Yet we all have a hand to lend!

Assignments & essays, grades and exams,
Emotion explosions as well,
Community living is life at its best
Comfort-zone erosions will tell!

No jeans in the classroom, no smoking or booze
No pyjamas downstairs of course,
When asked to help how can you refuse,
In this place of harmonious peace?

For ninety percent of us it's home from home,
Therefore escape is not wise,
For tho' the desire is to run off and roam,
God has His plans to devise!

And speaking of God, let's not leave Him out -
This is His place after all,
He brought each one of us here, no doubt,
Let's trust Him and honour the call!

There Was a Petrol Crisis

Life is a car......
well we'll say it is today,
it's what you are - or what you make of it, 'they' say,

Automobiles......
what kind would you select?
Spacious, practical or sporty with rollbars to protect?

Ah yes! about the fuel......
(If OPEC bans Arabian oil
then you'd better ride a mule) What stops engine-boil?

Prayer does.......*Selah* **- now think on this:**

wherever you are going
prayer will get you there,
driving fast, or slowing, all need daily fills of prayer.

There are no queues for praying,
no double prices paying,
and even more good news folks
prayer is certainly no hoax!
don't let the enemy blockade you
or stop the prayer trucks rolling.

Don't hide your prayers in the back - with the spares -
pray right round the steering wheel;
don't try to run on 'empty' or let an over-busy day distract,
we have an ever flowing source to tap,
use it always - it's your best road map.
Selah **- now think on this**
the vehicle is nothing......it's the fuel we can't live without!

New Year's Eve

The atmosphere around the ward
that was my working place
left much, that night, to be desired,
sadness and pain etched on each face.

The over-zealous heating vied
with unpleasant odours, plus
heady perfume at each bedside
their blooms a colour splash.

The TV news showed snowy views
and warned of icy blasts
then outside, through open'd blinds
we saw thick flakes falling fast.

Like feathers from a broken pillow
those fat flakes came tumbling down
dancing in the lamplight's goldglow
settling silently on the ground.

Next morning dawned was New Year's Eve,
bright sun on dazzling white;
a walk, as old year took its leave,
before next duty shift, seemed right.

Up on the Downs the bitter cold
was by us & dogs alike ignored,
shrieks of fun and rides on sleds
by children who for more implored.

Yet those old dears in hospice beds
who'd seen the snowflakes fall
could only toss & turn their heads
and let the past enthrall.

Do-Be

No, that's not the start of something famous Frank once sang
nor is it a misquote of William's well known question,
though to-be-or-not is a part of what is on my mind.
Why is it so hard for us
to simply be instead of do?
The Bible says be doers not just hearers of the Word;
and as women we were raised to do for others, everything.
Another childhood guilt trip when sitting down to rest is
'satan finds some mischief still
for idle hands to do',
implying that we're only good
when doing all there is to do.
These learned behaviour patterns are very hard to change;
in fact they're very useful to hide behind, like masks,
for as long as we keep doing there is no time to ask.....
if perhaps the Lord would have
us choose a better way;
for the Bible also says we should
be still, be still and know
that God is God, a fact
which gets squeezed out of doing.
And yes, in simply being we right away grow calm
and there is time and space to hear His voice in any storm;
of course some doings must get done
but oh just being is so much more fun!

Rejected

How could I ever have wasted a moment of
precious time communing with You Lord?

Reinstated,
Re-claimed,
Revitalised,
Redeemed,
Revamped,
Restored, Renewed,
Revived.....

No longer a duty, no longer a chore
Now I'm crying Lord, crying for more......

Without any warning You took my heart,
There it was cracking, breaking apart......

Embarrassment first, being seen by others,
Suddenly I thirst as I'm seen by You......oh God......

Make me want to pray, Lord, sensing Your response
Never let me waste a moment, make me want to pray......

Psalm 86

Incline Your ear O Lord I pray
Give me an undivided heart
Let me give You my love today
For You alone are God!

Teach me Your ways O Lord I pray
Give me an undivided heart
Teach me to walk within Your way
For You alone are God!

Help me to understand I pray
A glimpse of all Your wondrousness
Unite my heart to fear Your Name
For You alone are God!

Help us to tell the world we pray
Uniting undivided hearts
'Till all the nations praise Your Name
For You alone are God! Hallelujah! Hallelujah!

No Pie In The Sky

Fidgety but flightless
boxed and boisterous
itching for independence
watching from wicker windows......
billing, cooing, jostling, settling, scrabbling,
tensing, stretching, waiting, knowing......flexing for freedom

at *just the right time* the fancier loosens latches, drops doors, releasing

frenetic flapping feathers
forming themselves into mobile artistry
swooping, climbing, diving, soaring, wheeling
one graceful group circling into deep oceans of air
highlighting such limits on mere groundlings......
highlighting new meaning in 'just' being bird-brained......

how do they do it, these his avian treasures?
By staying close 'til they find their line, then disappearing
on direct homing instinct, always returning to the point of liberation.

Oh! earthbound friends, please recognise
humanity is also made to soar (unaided by metallic wings)
once quickened by The Fancier's saving grace, loosed, set free
just at the right time, we can reach the very heart of God......

How do we do it? By staying close, always returning
to the Cross - our point of liberation. We are His treasures,
and He's placed His homing instinct inside each one of us!

The Crux of the Matter

FROM CHILDHOOD SUNDAY
SCHOOL TO CONFIRMATION
CLASSES, HYMNS, BIBLE
READING AND OF COURSE
THE EASTER STORY, MOST
FOLK GROW UP KNOWING
AT LEAST SOMETHING OF
YOUR CROSS LORD EVEN IF
IT'S ONLY A SYMBOLIC
SHAPE TO GRACE THE NECK,
EMBOSS THE BOOK OF COMMON PRAYER AND SIT ON TOP OF STEEPLES, JUST
REPRESENTING THOSE 'RELIGIOUS NUTS' WHO LIKE TO GO TO CHURCH. LORD
HELP ME TO REALIZE AND BEGIN TO UNDERSTAND A LITTLE MORE EACH DAY
OF ALL THE IMPLICATIONS, WHAT IT MUST HAVE COST YOU, THE HURT & PAIN AND
LONELINESS, THAT CUT-OFF-FROM-GOD DARK HELL YOU ENDURED, BLAMELESSLY,
WILLINGLY, THOUGH YOU PRAYED TO BE RELEASED YOU STILL AGREED TO DO IT.
THEY DID NOT TAKE YOUR
LIFE YOU GAVE IT FREELY
STRETCHED OUT HANGING
THERE IN AGONY UNTIL
IT WAS FINISHED. O GOD
YOU LET YOUR SON DO THAT
FOR ME. PLEASE TEACH
ME TO APPRECIATE IN
EVERY SENSE MORE FULLY
THE VASTNESS OF THE
PRICE YOU PAID. YOU BROKE
THE POWER OF DEATH AND
SATAN'S EVIL SCHEMES
FOR ME, SO THAT I CAN
NOW KNOW LIFE AND
KNOW IT SO MUCH MORE
ABUNDANTLY AND LIVE
IN YOU AND YOU IN ME.
LORD JESUS WHEN I SURVEY
THIS VERY CROSS, EMPTY
NOW, THE BRIDGE FOR ME
TO CROSS FROM EARTH
TO HEAVEN, I THANK YOU.
YOUR OFFERING OF LIFE,
YOURS UPON THE CROSS
FOR MINE ETERNALLY,
ACCEPT MY THANKS IN MY
ACCEPTANCE OF YOUR GIFT.

Inflation

Bobbing about, in size varieties,
or helium filled, firm anchored to a base,
egos and balloons hold similarities.

Blown up for parties, birthdays celebrated,
full of self-importance, ready to impress
but fragile, oh so easily deflated.

With post-occasion wilt they shrink, collapse,
hopes and dreams escape, slowly evaporate
leaving useless empty has-beens......perhaps

like automobile airbags, we're too keen
to be inflated full of pride's hot air,
forgetting it can maim though unforeseen;

and a football, if roughly toe'd and heel'd
rips when overkicked, never reaching goal -
pigskin left lying limply in the field.

When I'm full inflated with me-itis
Lord burst my bubble, gently, then refill,
re-infect again with pure You-itis.

Oh God Your Breath of Life breathe into me
with a sufficiency of You to share
let me expand to full capacity.

Fruit Stealers

Ripe melons, peaches, apples, plums, displayed for all to see, are yours for cash, or, with sticky thumbs some folk would thieving be.

But different kinds, non-edible, cannot be bought and sold, hard to learn, though obtainable, more value to young and old......

Self-control, peace, patience, kindness, the list is still much longer, love, goodness, joy and faithfulness will really make you stronger.

Yet with the strength must gentleness be mixed - proportions even, for one without the other seems like bread without the leaven.

Lord, help me grow my fruit supply, please polish, hone and ripen, protect from frost and satan's lie, guard all from being stolen.

Christmas

If you remove the booze, the drugs, the glitter,
you will be called 'no fun,' boring, bitter,
if you decline to drink their wine only they will suffer - you'll be fitter!
If you concentrate on pressies, cards & cash
doing all to help dear Santa's headlong dash......
(she sent to me so don't you see I'll send her this from last year's stash.)
If you buy gifts because you feel you ought
is it any wonder that your shopping's fraught?
If you decorate but really hate the season-*stop*-think what were you taught:
where exactly in the Bible does it say
a word of snowmen, reindeer or a sleigh?
Not a mention of festive convention just angels, star, shepherds, manger and hay.
Hhhmmmm......
We over-eat and over-spend in over-expectation
we over-wrap and over-dress in over-admiration
of each other, when 'why bother?' is far more honest, minus the libation.
Strip it all away and what's remaining? Room enough to bring Christ back
and have Him reigning? Christ in Christmas - Oh my gracious!
Yes *that's* the real point, and we can see the real meaning.
Let's get on our knees (not just a church activity)
and thank our God for Christ His Son's Nativity
about Whose birth there can be no passivity;
then can be seen and felt true celebration
for those who love the Lord a frequent occupation
because He came to birth for us
to birth in us new Life and total adoration!

Beach Grace

Pearly grey gave in to blue, four hours before nine,
pale Luna sailed away, stripping stars of shine;
I walked the dawn, head down, shell-seeking
in the glistening ebb, wet soles squelching.
Sandy wavelets inching back to their allotted place
mindful of not transgressing His command.
Heaving greeny depths transporting from the land
to navy horizontal so dark against the newday sky.
Heralded by red-topped clouds, the upper crescent
of Your sun raised itself into full round magnificence.

"...and then I saw what seemed to be a glassy sea blended with fire."
(Rev 15:2)

Irregular dissecting groyne lines lifting praises
from each post - a perch for solitary gulls -
each bird, aimed at the morning, some silent,
some, craws wide, singing like the song of Moses......

"Mighty and marvellous are Your works O Lord..." - (Rev 15:4)

Is that how we shall be Lord when You return -
some silent, some praising as we behold Your glory?
Including those who, gull-ish, try to run away
stiff-legged and kneeless...... yet we know
that at Your Name each and every knee will bow.
That fiery eastern orb now risen high, it's path
of glassy glare still impossible to gaze upon.
My eyes slide round to safer southern angle as
discordant screeches announce breakfast-on-the-wing,
harmonising with symphony of wind and waves.

Restful perfection to accompany my reverie, and my magnificat of praise
to You O God...... (Luke 1:46)

Take His Hand

Because you are a child of God
It doesn't mean it's easy
To tread the paths that He has trod
While smiling bright and breezy!

In fact it could be said for sure
It's far harder than you think
To keep afloat, eyes still on His,
Just hang on, swim, don't sink.

If in your own strength this you hope
To manage, well, you never will;
That's why you must give Him the job
Take His hand to climb each hill.

The best part is you're not alone
Tho' you can't see Him there
He's promised, even while you moan,
He is with you, never fear!

That's the meaning of His grace
It's His strength filling you,
His guidance leads in every race,
His wisdom shining through!

Windsurfing

Cold and grey, blustery;
In between hail storms
Silver sun emerges buffing dull pewter scene to celestial patina.
Retreating tide leaving a wealth
Of shells in its wake;
Horizon fuzzed in spume,
Surf high and messy
Only inviting two intrepid boarders - one with sail attached -
He knows how to ride the waves
Jump and leap and fly above the troubles,
He knows where his strength comes from
He is welded to his support system.

Over the rock pools slipping on seaweed,
Astonished to find I'm nearly at the estuary -
Turn back along the shore into the wind and sun,
Into a paean of praise for the Creator God, my own personal support.

Jeremiah 1:4-9

Before you were, I was
Before you were, I planned
Before you were, I knew you
And I set you apart for Me!

You are selected, appointed by Me
You are so cherished - more than you see
Don't say you cannot because you're afraid
I am beside you - you who I made
I'm close to rescue, I'll never depart
Be brave for Me child - heart of My heart
Go where I send you, say what I command
I will uplift you - take hold of my hand!

Before you were, I was
Before you were, I planned
Before you were, I knew you
And I set you apart for Me!

Woman At The Well

O woman, any, every, woman -
It matters not the country of your birth -
Raised to anticipate a wedding
And on it hang the level of your worth.

Expectantly you wait, then fall in love,
All feels secure as often many schemes
When set to flourish; but, excluding God,
Turn to disappointments, broken dreams.

Sometimes 'he' is the one and only
But sometimes several more will follow on,
Happiness shines briefly on each pairing
Then hurt and sadness ending every one.

Unrequited love is deeply painful,
Leaving bitter memories and scars -
Yet with Jesus we can learn to trust again
Lifting eyes and hearts towards the stars!

I used to think my value and my joy
Depended on a husband, partner, friend,
Now I know they come from God my Saviour
And He'll stay with me to the very end.

Circumstances cause me to live alone
But mine's the choice how best to do it -
Rather than gaze inward, I want to tell
Others what He's done for me, and show it!

Lessons from a Lump

I found a lump Lord. In my breast.
Instantly it formed another lump
Much bigger, made of lead,
That settled in my stomach with a nasty heavy thump.

I found a lump Lord. In my breast.
Bubbles everywhere and steam
Standing in the shower shampooing
I saw my altered contour -looked away, hoped it was a dream.

I found a lump Lord. In my breast.
It is not a dream, it's really there
A moment ever etched in time
Is it cancer? Will surgeon's knife remove it, or will it take my life?

I found a lump Lord. In my breast.
It may of course be only harmless cyst
In either case I know You're testing me
Do I believe what often I tell others, that You died for this, to set us free?

I found a lump Lord. In my breast.
Freedom is completely trusting You
Accepting that You are in control
Surrendering my life, and lump, to You as from it You'll bring good somehow.

I found a lump Lord. In my breast.
Thank You for the power of Your healing!
No, the lump has not gone, but instead
You've shown me again what I need to see, Your love in my heart and my head.

My Anchor

As the old hymn trills, 'Will your anchor hold?'
Yes, of course it will, I reply, quite bold.

My Anchor is fine, He will never fail,
The problem is mine - I've turned quite pale.

Links disconnected in the chain I see......
That's why I floundered, it's not Him but me.

Storms overwhelming, blowing me away
So, re-connecting is a must today.

An Hour One Morning

A grey parade of softly rolling elephants
marched along the treeline silently trumpeting,
ruined the sunrise - though magnificent themselves,
billowing taller they grew, quietly thunderous,
changing their shapes, thickening their intensity......
reinforcements from the north moved down to eat
more colour, consume the early glow, reducing
radiance to dull, turning warmth to autumn chill.

Sudden transformation! From source as yet unseen
pours rosy sheen, backlighting elephantine tops,
igniting conflagrations, oh marvellous artistry!
Accumulated cumuli have met their match,
now quenched with liquid gold, retreat, shrink, disperse,
still gilded, in awe, they bow before their Maker
Who spreads more rays up through their fading forms
re-painting all with fiery fresh magnificence.

Up From The Pit

Clutched at and chilled
by fingers of fear
surrounded by
smothering sadness
I've lain awake
listening to lies
dreamt dreams
round reality
switched off symptoms
(shaking and sobbing)
to coax conviviality
and dispel despair
is this a breakdown
or a batch of bad days
illogical illness or
logical lethargy
longing for lighthearted
handfuls of health
rejoicing, revitalising
singing songs in the sun
paeans of praise.

Weights and Measures

I once had a fine *collection* of old and antique scales that took much time
to polish and required space to display. What was the great *attraction?*
Balance was never my thing, Too often dizzy and always busy
measuring outward appearance. I needed more *concentration*
for weighing up life itself: overdependence on one side or
independence too strong. Where is the *centralisation,*
sweet oil of interdependence? Jesus please be
my linchpin and help my stability too.
Now I've sold the *collection*
re-focused the *attraction,*
improved *concentration*
and *centralisation*
under Your
direction.
Just a
moment, I
can't leave it there
without adding one
weight onto the flat plate
or into the brass pan because now
I can see the need for the seed of God's
Word that I've heard to *balance* with His
Spirit oh there is so much in it! But I do not want
to dry up nor most certainly blow up with too much of
one and not enough of the other. Lord, please guide me I
pray to grow up more each day with my sisters and brothers
help us all to discern as together we learn deeper *concentration* on You
the *attraction,*we need to be wise and to *centralise* on You Jesus Christ, amen.

Seasonal Praise

Yes, the leaves have gone

Fluttering away their golden ruby wealth

Impoverished bare branches left

But no, not for long!

Now, after rain, transformed again,

Draped like ancient dowager necks

In dazzling diamond droplets

Crystal clear, festooned, and poised

To catch the first of early morning sun -

Unvalued riches, uninsured,

Requiring neither bank nor vault.

Soon to change, in lower climes,

Sparkling still, but solid then

To ice shapes undesignable

By human hand, only our Creator can

And He waits a few months yet

To clothe His trees with spring's new green -

Pale emeralds' trembling lace.

Swans

A scene of heartbreak met my gaze
down by the river in yesterday's
spring sun. The swan sat half submerged
as rushing tide in full spate urged
all before it, twigs and reeds -
our pen with stretched neck knew her needs
she beaked the bits into her nest
in desperation doing her best
to stem the flow and save her eggs
still anchored twixt her breast and legs
how tirelessly she fought the fight
protecting unborn cygnets' right
to hatch and grow, spread waterwings,
learn river life with all it brings
and when their turn comes to make a home
teach them to build high, out of harm!
Faithfully swans pair up for life
better than many a man and wife,
but that cob tactlessly looked on,
selfish he seemed, floating along
preening, flexing majestic wings
sparkling spraying arcs he flings
with abandon across his back,
how can he play? She must attack
the rising death, fend off the flood
threatening their precious brood.

Nocturnal Yearnings

Sleep eludes, tension mounts, I'm counting
days and hours, one week left, I'm packing
for the flight, longed-for trip: exciting!
USA and UK uniting......
unfolding miracle happening......
brand new babe, first time gran, wondering......
five thousand miles and heartstrings stretching......
Emma Elizabeth welcoming;
my grown son, now a dad, amazing!
All seems well, thank You Lord, I'm praising!

Faces

Lord is that You -
could it be
Your hands
cupping my face
lifting my head
speaking my name
so I lift my eyes
to look into Your face.
Or is it me -
averting
my gaze away from You
because between us
my burdens get
in the way blocking
my efforts to see You
oh Jesus help -
let it be
us looking face to face
please lift my head
and speak my name
so I'll lift my eyes
to the love in Your face.

Psalm 145:13-16

Astrocytoma

It's growing
No one can stop it
Growing fast inside his head
Pressing in on important bits
Turning his leg to lead.

It's eating
Eating away at his life
Clouding his sparkle, tolling its knell,
Watched by his heart-breaking wife.

I want to
Open his skull
Scoop it out with a spoon
Repair and revitalise
Make it all better soon.

I want to
See a miraculous healing
Or be there as God calls him home
Watch his face shine - Jesus revealing.

Farewell To A Friend

It's the final delegation, last journey. Dying as you lived - neatly.
The light has left your eyes; just a shell upon the pillow now......

Stripped of your own pyjamas, clad in a hospital gown,
injection to reduce secretions, help the coughing......
Life on the ward carries on as it always does;
my colleagues try to whisper, cut the banter down,
but the deaf need shouting to, the lame need wheels
nearby, a nebuliser hisses medicated breath into
tortured lungs, a pegasus bed's motor drones on,
dressings need changing as many a wound heals.

Intermittent buzz as the pump pushes morphine round your body,
sudden spasms interrupt peaceful breathing......

Irregular twitch of a finger as I hold your hand on the sheet,
Dear friend, it's time to let go, please let go......

Lord, have You already taken him? Has he seen Your face?
Has he reached Your outstretched arms of welcome?
Does he hear Your words, "Well done, thou good and
faithful servant!" Or is he still locked into that dark place
of confusion, frustration, cranial pressure and pain?
The accuser's still trying to drag him, but Jesus You are the
Victor in the battle, already victorious Almighty God,

You know why, when and how of earthly death, then the gain
of heaven! Oh Lord, release him, please release him soon.

DLJ August '98 at VHL.

Titus 3:5

The Pharisee & the Tax Collector
were standing side by side
the first one thought he was so good
the second hung his head & cried.

This parable's in Luke eighteen
in ninth to fourteenth verse
that overconfident Pharisee
was, in God's eyes much worse

Than the Taxman who knew his sins
were bad as bad could be,
knew he needed the mercy of God
Before he could look up & be free.

So let this be a lesson to all
of us who think we're great,
look honestly at what we're really like
& ask forgiveness before it's too late.

We are only saved by God's mercy
not by our good deeds or merit,
so it's up to us to accept His offer -
eternal life - it's ours to inherit.

Millennium

Nothing in all of Christendom
Equals the Birth that gives us cause
To celebrate in maximum!
Jesus we give You our applause
Forgive our pandemonium
We long for ending of all wars
And answers to mysterium
How soon will open Heaven's doors
Then we'll see ad infinitum
And want to praise You more because
This is Your own Millenium......
This is Your own Millenium!

Singleness

Deut. 13:3 The Lord your God is testing you to find out whether you love Him with all your heart and all your soul......

Yes, Lord with all my heart and soul I love You totally and it's so very
good to know You feel the same about me,
I'm in love with the King of kings and He's in love with me!
But I don't like singleness Lord, I'm lonesome - achingly
It would be good to have a spouse - someone dear to me
To touch skin to skin without any impropriety
To cherish and be cherished, to be valued lovingly
Down here on earth, for the last years before eternity.
But it honestly doesn't matter, realistically
I'm in love with the King of kings and He's in love with me!
I'm not complaining Lord, I've managed since nineteen ninety
If marriage isn't in Your plan I'll still manage...... cheerfully
With You beside me step by step trusting continually......
Seeking no more Ishmaels, I'll wait contentedly
For only the Isaac of Your choice, and he will, upon his knee
Confess that even more than me he loves You completely
And he too will lift his hands and sing most worshipfully
'I'm in love with the King of kings and He's in love with me.'

I can't just sit and wait around for You to meet my needs fulfillingly
Unless I agree it's a two-way deal, choosing acknowledgingly
You know what's best, know my desires, know me intimately
I'm in love with the King of kings and He's in love with me!

Thank you God that you are God and I am not - definitely!
I can trust you, lean on You, walk with You dependently,
In You I am whole, on my own, complete as is - amazingly!
I'm in love with the King of kings and He's in love with me!

Biblical Counselling

Satan cannot afford to have Eden restored -
that would bring order to home and to Church,
he would rather drive wedges and tear down the hedges
we build, and Christ's good Name besmirch.

Married couples *together* any storm they can weather,
while singles stand tall, complete as they are;
under God's direction all receive His protection,
uniting to stamp on the devil - hurrah!

Reconciling he hates, so let's open the gates
asking Jesus the Wonderful Counsellor in,
every counselling session can teach a good lesson
on facing each problem, forgiving each sin.

Once that is done do not dwell and be glum
thinking only of troubles, heartache and pain,
instead dwell on Jesus and all He's achieved for us -
you'll soon be rejoicing and praising again!

God's Word is a lamp - our lives to revamp,
tells how to resist Satan then watch him flee,
there wisdom we find and true peace of mind,
The Word's full of wise counsel for you and for me.

Remembrance Day

They say rosemary is for remembrance, but today its poppies red -
to remind us of the ones who died, who fought the wars,
who saved this land for us, and gave their lives instead.
When those soldiers went to war, willingly or not,
they knew the cost, they knew the pain, they knew the stakes were
high, and yet they still agreed to do it, to stand for us and die,
so that we can live in peace, and be set free
from fear, oppression, tyranny, from greed, and hate and sin.
Some say history is boring, all that was long ago,
why bother now to think of them? Just the oldies want to know,
so maybe once a year we'll sing a hymn and watch a TV show
of wreath-laying at the Cenotaph and rows of whitened graves.

Never will they fade away, we will remember them,
their sacrifice shall never wane throughout eternity.

But wait, all this remembering must surely bring to mind
the One Who did it first for us, Who knew the cost and pain
and yet He willingly laid down His life upon that Cross
raised high for all to see and jeer.
And still today are those who say
why bother now to think of Him? Maybe once a year
we'll go to church and sing a hymn - eat lots of turkey too
or quantities of hidden chocolate eggs.
But still they jeer because they do not see
that Jesus gave His life for us to be set free
from fear, oppression, tyranny, from greed and hate and sin.
Let Him in and find His peace, freedom, and be clean within.

Jesus for sure will never fade, His sacrifice goes on,
He's awaiting our decision - where will we spend eternity?

The A283 In Spring

Drive if needs must, but do not rush, allow safe glimpsing moments;
calming balm
for stress awaiting or just left behind.
Gentle delight of bluebell blue - nothing else can match that hue,
it carpets and beckons through wooded shade
urging you slow
breathe deep the fragrance.
Ditches daringly dandelion decorated yet mauve-swathed too
with pint-ed cuckoo.
Snowdrifting pale anemones gracefully slalom around tall trunks
while opposite,
a gilded glade of buttery cups and jaunty sunny celandines suddenly dulled:
harsh neon brilliance can only mean soon gleaned for oily profit,
a seeding field of ripening rape.
Glaring or soothing, light or shadow, tarmac overarched in
quivering lacy greenness, dainty filigree.
Occasionally interspersed with black beams on white, or ancient brick,
wonky rooves tile hung or thatched
propped up together side by side along the village curves.
Then comes a woolly flock, hefty pedigree,
four feet dug lushly into chlorophyll, grazing lazily
well matched by breezing clouds
as your four wheels ease past another patch of bluebell blue.
Dig this sight into your brain
keep secure for days of rain, fleeting heat and dull winter bare.

New Life

Gether = wine press............
Ancient tortured forms still grow - each olive tree
Bears witness to what happened there, Gethsemane
The very name means olive press, fruits must be crushed;
When I stood among those twisted trunks, the pale air was hushed.

Sema = sustained............
The name, from further root, is equal to sustained
So, only by power Divine, was my Lord tho' sorely pained,
Kept strong enough to see it through, the will of Father God obey
Bearing all my punishment and shame that I may freely Live today.

Hallel = praise............
Like Advent, Lent's thoughtful weeks, such time of preparation
To reflect upon Your birth, then death, then glorious resurrection!
May we, with saints of old, lift heart and voice in wonder and in praise,
In springtime's vital newness, resounding hallelujahs all our days!

A Glimpse Of God

Eternity... eternally... immeasurably
God before time, of time, for all time
explaining Himself in permanence
revealing Himself in simplicity
hiding Himself from no one
His magnificence reachable,
message understandable,
His truth available
His love visible......

stars poised in a dark velvet sky
wave washed stones on shore
ever changing
Abraham knew and we do too,
yesterday's rock fossils make
today's pebbles which are
tomorrow's grains of sand
ever changing
throughout His story God
the great I AM
never changing.

Here But Briefly

I will arise and go Home to my Father
While Jesus holds you close in His arms
Thank you for holding me thru' all the palava
Oh this is Gilead and yes there is balm!

Selah - pause and think on this

I am now fully completely well
The air is celestial filling my lungs
I can breathe deeply & chuckle & chatter
I'm wrapped in assurance from Jesus Himself
That He knows your pain, your wrenching sorrow
He's pouring in peace to soothe every heart.

He'll wipe all your tears as He has done mine
He'll carry your grief, He knows it's too heavy.
He's promised He'll never leave or forsake you
For He is your Refuge, your Tower of Strength.
I am safe here, Home with our Father and
He tells me you're safe, enfolded in Him.

A few words in attempt to contain all the sadness
But finding it crushing, too much to bear,
So opening clenched fingers to loosen the grip
Releasing it upwards in wordless prayer. Amen.

Rapturous

There can be few better ways
to worship You oh Lord, and praise
You for the gift of life & Your creation
than to climb the Downs watching day's cessation.
The Son who made the sun to light our days
must take the credit even as He takes the haze
as if with finger of divine hand leading through
the valleys, gathering layers of mist from greeny-blue
to purply-pink and wispy white along the river's oxbow bends.
Above that mist the eye is drawn once more,
fold upon fold, hills darkening though it's not yet four,
the gentle whale-back silhouette horizons
seeming to absorb the fiery gold emblazoned
on every cloud edge, then radiate it yonder
to double the effect & magnify the wonder.
Wet grasses & chill air of winter afternoon
do not deter, in fact enhance; I'm well cocooned
in boots, scarf & gloves, to stand awhile, leaning
on convenient fencepost, sorting out the meaning
of the words in Holy Writ concerning, Lord,
Your second visit here, when those of us who've heard
Your call will be caught up with You in clouds like these,
golden, filled with angel crowds singing far more beautifully
than I can now tho' heart is bursting, full of praise, and I bow
my soul, & my whole life to You Lord, at Your feet,
as I call the dog, my faithful friend & together we
turn for home, sunset safely in my mind, for tea.